HOW DO YOU TURN IT ON?

by
Bil Keane

A Fawcett Gold Medal Book

FAWCETT GOLD MEDAL • NEW YORK

A Fawcett Gold Medal Book
Published by Ballantine Books
Copyright © 1985, 1980 by Register and Tribune Syndicate, Inc.

Library of Congress Catalog Card Number: 85-90610

ISBN 0-449-12421-5

Printed in Canada

First Ballantine Books Edition: June 1985
Sixth Printing: March 1989

"Can't wait till I'm grown up and I can do
anything I want and not have anything
to worry about."

"Well, PJ, I can't find Dolly and Jeffy
ANYWHERE. I suppose we might as well
go without them."

"If they 'member who you are, then you're a member."

"Here are the two eggs Mommy borrowed.
Are you gonna tell her I dropped one?"

"But I TRIED to tell him we'd only be gone
for a little while!"

"Look at the task force of ducks!"

"If Mommy hadn't married Daddy, we'd be
in some other family."

"Know why PJ doesn't talk so good? I sink
it's 'cause he's too yittle."

"This soft stuff around the outside is called peach fudge."

"Look! A passenger swing."

"Daddy says prime time is when the best shows are on."
"See? I TOLD you it was Saturday morning."

"I know what a puff is. But what's a huff?"

"Mommy didn't think it was that funny when I said it this afternoon. I had to go to my room."

"I'm sure we're in for a storm. I'm looking
right at the barometer."

"They flash the lightning to warn you that the thunder is coming."

"Aren't your eyes empty yet?"

"Let's hurry up and decide, Dolly. I'm cold."

"Will you take me to see another rainbow
someday, Mommy?"

"Listen to this, God, here's an offer you can't refuse."

"They're not sending me to the showers. I'm just going to the bathroom."

"Somebody crayoned on that man's arm."

"My bike will really feel skinny after this!"

"Neither of us can read yet."

"I AM gettin' washed, but right now I'm in the soak cycle."

"I've gotta go to the bathroom. I'm putting
you on hold."

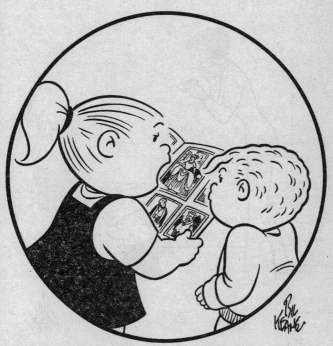

"People who don't have any children don't get
to be ancestors."

"Wonder if there's enough energy in this candy bar to bring the old newspapers up from the basement and carry out the trash?"

"Aw, Mommy — Popeye can't eat spinach.
He's just a cartoon."

"How come my reflection is lefthanded?"

"Where does he keep the pork chops?"

"Just don't look down through the cracks."

"Mommy! You've got bikini shoes, too!"

"Now I have my own picture window."

"Mommy! PJ is taking his pants off just because
they're wet!"

"So the basketball would go through it."

"Let me sit there, Daddy?"

"Wonder why they named her Joy?"

"Why does that ham have tacks in it?"

"September already! Y'know, Daddy, the
days really fly by when you
get to be seven."

"The hardest part about goin' back to
school is learning how to whisper again."

"I'm glad we don't have to change mothers
every year the way we change teachers."

"You're too little to use deodorant, Jeffy.
You haven't even learned to sweat yet."

"Who put in this box
of candy bars?"

"Not me!"
"Not me!"

"He's busy sleeping."

"Aren't I old enough to carry my lunch in a
brown paper bag?"

"Our Daddy desserted us. Mommy cooked
dinner and Daddy desserted
us with ice cream."

"Ha, ha! Your wish won't come true. You
made it on an airplane light."

"Now, remember — I want you to behave."
"Don't worry, Mommy, I'll be REAL 'haive'."

"Run it backwards again, Daddy, and unjump me."

"It's a roll of inches."

"Jack and Jill, Jack and the Beanstalk, Jack Be
Nimble, Jack Spratt . . . were all Mother
Goose's friends named Jack?"

"I wish I had some homework for you
to help me with."

"Miss McElfresh says we should eat lots of
protein, Mommy. Why don't
you ever buy any?"

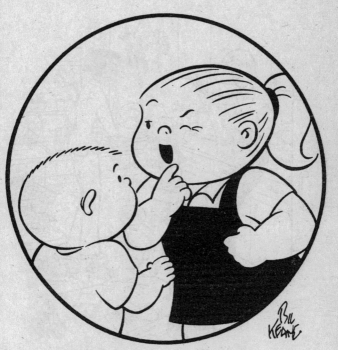

"See? A wink is half a blink."

"Sometimes I wonder why we bought
a seven-room house."

"Daddy, why don't you push the little red
line back from E?"

"When I grow up and have kids how would you
like the job as grandparents?"

"Eat your food, Barfy. Think of all the starving doggies all over the world."

"Mommy, will you make PJ
turn down his volume?"

"Why are you feeling our
toothbrushes, Mommy?"

"One of the teachers had a baby and brought him to school today for Show-and-Tell."

"Mommy, I think some of Daddy's things
got in my drawer."

"The only place he got hurt is in his feelings."

"Billy's been made TV critic for the school newspaper."

"Did you bring us anything?"

"Have I been good today?"

"Why don't we get a compact car, Daddy?"

"Is there 'fast motion'? Or just 'regular motion' and 'slow motion'?"

"Billy's talkin' about the birds and the bees. Is that naughty?"

"I spoiled my appetite with dinner."

"Greg's mother is divorced from his real daddy,
and she has a step-husband now."

"You know you're in trouble when she starts off
'Young man. . . .'"

"Who ate the ice cream off those sticks?"

"I'll throw a pass to Dolly this time. PJ, you
block Daddy."

"These are called place maps 'cause they show
you where your place is."

"My teacher gave me a hug today. Is that all
right with you?"

"Kiss Daddy on the other cheek. I just kissed him on that one."

"Can I drive now, Mommy?"

"Daddy, can I draw on this piece of your
giraffe paper?"

"Daddy, what's a football widow?"

"Mommy's going to dress a letter. Wanna watch her do it?"

"I know A, B, C, G, D, H . . . but I don't know
what comes next."

"Will you write a letter to me some day,
Mommy, so I can get some mail, too?"

"Mommy would never divorce Daddy. He's just like one of the family."

"I think my rake has to be flossed."

"They called your number, Mommy! What do we win?"

"Which one am I?"

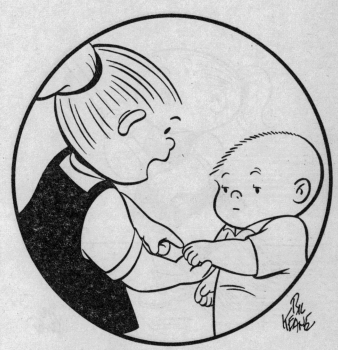

"All these little elbows are called knuckles."

"Mommy, this broom is going bald."

"Daddy's tired, but we're not. Can you go out
with us now?"

"I hope we're not votin' for HIM. He pre-empted our cartoons!"

"The trees are going blank."

"My mommy's votin' for . . . mmmph!"

"A lot of the guys' mothers type their book reports for them."

"These letters aren't even in alphabetical order!"

"Do you know who Zeus is?"
"Sure, he's a doctor and he writes stories for kids."

"Wanna see something funny, Daddy? Cross your legs."

"Listen, Mommy! It's the theme song from that
program you and Daddy watch
on Sunday nights."

"Look at that squirrel on the wire. He's
pretending he's a tightrope walker."

"Mommy! How old do you hafta be before
they can send you to jail?"

"If he was in a story like Rabbits Rafferty
he'd be able to talk to us."

"I'll save your seat
for you, Mommy."

"It's a good thing kids are washable!"

"Barfy's taking PJ for a walk."

"Guess who my name is?"

"Get your milk off there, P.J. Don't you know
this is a COFFEE table?"

"We better not sit there, Mommy. This
lady's smoking."

"Wow! Those logs must have firecrackers
in them."

"Watch it, Billy, or I'll give you a black nose."

"Hi, Grandma! Remember me?"

"Which do you want to do first, Grandma —
crayon or play cards?"

"When you use this bathroom, Grandma, you
hafta jiggle the handle to make
the toilet stop running."

"You're sayin' grace with your eyes open, Billy!
I saw you!"

"We hafta wait till granddad listens to his old
Larry Clinton records."

"All you and Granddad have done is talk and
drink tea. When's your VACATION
gonna start?"

"I like it when grandma and granddad are here. We can each have a grown-up."

"Are you awake yet, Grandma? Or are you
still asleep?"

"Daddys take you for runs and drives, but granddads take you for walks."

"Let's walk down this street, Granddad. We'll
pass the Sugar Bowl, a toy store,
a doughnut shop. . . ."

"Then what ELSE did mommy do when she was
a little girl?"

"I'll send you a letter, Grandma — as soon as I learn to write."

"Get up, Mommy! There's a surprise all over
the neighborhood!"

"Jeffy? . . . PJ? . . ."

"Between the dark and daylight,
        When the night is beginning to lower,
Comes a pause in the day's occupation
        That is known as the children's hour."